A Zondervan/Ladybird Bible Book

# Jesus the Storyteller

By Jenny Robertson
Illustrated by Alan Parry

## ZONDERVAN
### PUBLISHING HOUSE
OF THE ZONDERVAN CORPORATION
GRAND RAPIDS, MICHIGAN 49506

2

Jesus told many stories. Here is one about a shepherd who loved his sheep. The shepherd would come into the sheepfold, call their names, and lead them away to the best pastures. Sometimes thieves would try to steal the sheep, and fierce wolves would attack the flock, but the shepherd would protect them, however great the danger.

"I am like that good shepherd," said Jesus. "The people who follow Me are like the sheep. I know them and they know Me. I look after them, and I give My life to keep them safe."

3

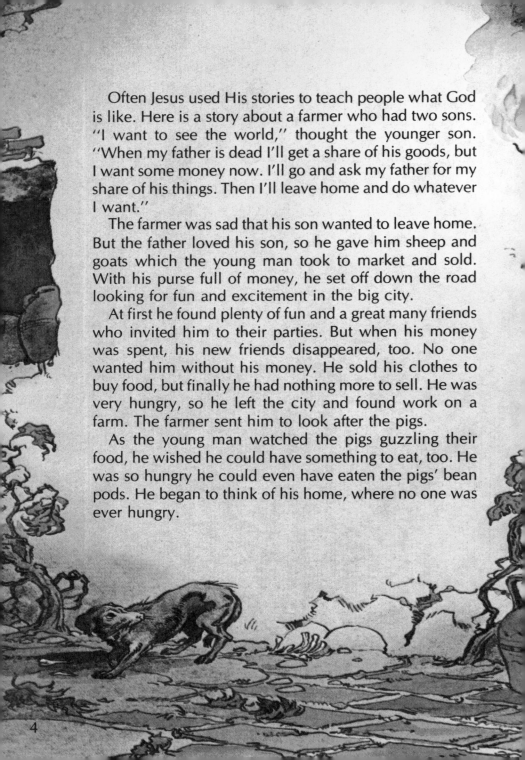

Often Jesus used His stories to teach people what God is like. Here is a story about a farmer who had two sons. "I want to see the world," thought the younger son. "When my father is dead I'll get a share of his goods, but I want some money now. I'll go and ask my father for my share of his things. Then I'll leave home and do whatever I want."

The farmer was sad that his son wanted to leave home. But the father loved his son, so he gave him sheep and goats which the young man took to market and sold. With his purse full of money, he set off down the road looking for fun and excitement in the big city.

At first he found plenty of fun and a great many friends who invited him to their parties. But when his money was spent, his new friends disappeared, too. No one wanted him without his money. He sold his clothes to buy food, but finally he had nothing more to sell. He was very hungry, so he left the city and found work on a farm. The farmer sent him to look after the pigs.

As the young man watched the pigs guzzling their food, he wished he could have something to eat, too. He was so hungry he could even have eaten the pigs' bean pods. He began to think of his home, where no one was ever hungry.

"My father is kind and treats everyone well, even the servants," he thought. "How stupid I am, sitting here starving! I'll go back home. I'll tell my father I'm sorry."

The more he thought about it, the better the idea seemed. He planned what he would say: "Father, I've done wrong. I've treated you badly and I've done wrong in God's eyes, too. I'm not fit to be your son any more. Please take me back as one of your servants."

Feeling happier than he had been for a long time, the young man started home to his father.

Some time later, when his father was looking out of the window, he spotted a ragged figure, limping along. The farmer stared. Then he raced down the dusty road and flung his arms around his son. The son started to say how sorry he was, but the farmer hurried into the house with him, overjoyed to have him home again.

"Bring the best robe and put it on my son," he called to the servants. "Give him a ring to wear, and sandals, too. Kill the young calf. We'll have a splendid feast!"

God is like the kind father in this story. He forgives those who are sorry for the wrong things they have done and who come back to Him.

Another story Jesus told was about two very different men who went to pray in the temple.

The first man was a Pharisee, who thought he always kept God's laws. He swept proudly in through the temple doors and stood where everyone could see him. Loudly he told God how good he was. "Thank You, God, that I'm better than other people. I'm not like that tax collector there. I do everything that pleases You."

The tax collector, who had come very quietly into the temple, bent his head lower and whispered, "Have pity on me, God. I've done wrong and I'm sorry."

Both men went home, but God forgave the tax collector, and not the Pharisee.

Jesus told the story to teach His friends that God is more pleased with those who know they have done wrong and admit it, than with those who think they are good but look down on others.

"If you follow My teaching you are like the wise man who built his house on rock," said Jesus.

"First he dug away the sandy soil. Then he built his house. When the rain flooded the valley and autumn storms shook the house, it stood firm, for it was built solidly right on the rock.

"Another man built a house nearby, but he didn't dig right down to the rock. So when the valley was flooded, the sandy soil was washed away. The house creaked and shook in the autumn storms and came crashing down.

"Those who don't follow my teaching are like that," finished Jesus. "They can never stand firm when troubles come."

Here is a story which Jesus told about a robbery.

A traveler journeyed along a lonely road which wound through hills where bands of robbers hid. A gang of thieves attacked him, snatched his bags, stripped off his clothes, and beat him up. Then they ran away, leaving the man badly hurt. He would certainly die if no one helped him, but who would stop on such a dangerous road to help an injured man?

15

It happened that someone did come along, a priest, on his way to pray to God in the temple. He saw the man, but he was too frightened to stop. Quickly he walked away on the other side of the road.

Later on, the wounded man heard footsteps. He was too weak to shout, but whoever came by would see him. "Surely this person will help?" he thought, as the footsteps came closer.

The passer-by was on his way to serve God in the temple, too. He looked at the man for a moment, but then he crossed the road as well. He went on his way, leaving the hurt man lying by the road in the hot sun.

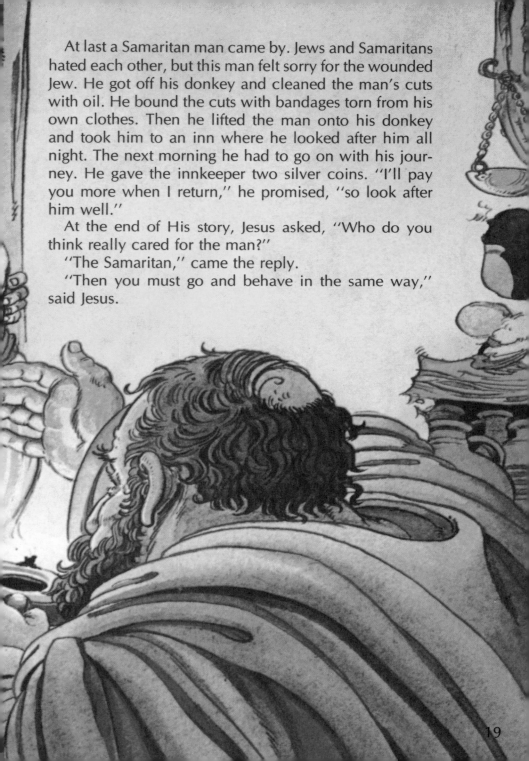

At last a Samaritan man came by. Jews and Samaritans hated each other, but this man felt sorry for the wounded Jew. He got off his donkey and cleaned the man's cuts with oil. He bound the cuts with bandages torn from his own clothes. Then he lifted the man onto his donkey and took him to an inn where he looked after him all night. The next morning he had to go on with his journey. He gave the innkeeper two silver coins. "I'll pay you more when I return," he promised, "so look after him well."

At the end of His story, Jesus asked, "Who do you think really cared for the man?"

"The Samaritan," came the reply.

"Then you must go and behave in the same way," said Jesus.

"Don't worry or be anxious," Jesus told His friends. "God will give you everything you need. Did you ever see a flower sit down to spin its beautiful dress? Of course not! Yet see how beautifully the flowers grow. Look at the purple anemones, the crocuses, the lovely lilies. Even the wealthiest king of all, King Solomon, who wore splendid robes of deep purple, never put on anything as lovely as what one wild flower wears. Look at the grass, starred with flowers one day, and withered the next. God dresses the ground so wonderfully that He will be certain to give you clothes and food, too. So why don't you just believe that? Expect God to look after you and stop worrying all the time!"

This is another story that Jesus told.

A farmer set out early one morning to sow his seed. He dipped his hand into the bag he carried and scattered the seed over the ground.

Some seed fell on the path. Birds flew down at once and pecked it up before it could grow on the hard, sun-baked earth of the pathway.

Some seed fell into stony earth where there was only a thin layer of soil. Young shoots sprang up very quickly, but they did not take root in the shallow earth. As soon as the hot sun rose, the tiny plants dried up and died.

Some of the seed fell among thorns which choked the shoots so that they could not grow.

Some seed, though, fell into good soil where it grew and ripened and stood thick and tall. When the harvest came, the farmer was happy, for the good ground gave back thirty, sixty, even a hundred times more corn than he had sown. It was a wonderful harvest!

What a good story, and what a wonderful harvest! But there was a secret meaning which Jesus explained to His friends. "The seed is our message about God. Remember the hard path? That's like the hearts of some people who never understand what we tell them."

Jesus went on, "Other people do understand and are thrilled with the message, but they don't want to do anything too hard. They are like the stony soil with only a thin layer of good earth; when trouble comes they give up easily, blaming God. Some people hear our message but all sorts of worries about money and the problems of everyday life grow up in their minds, too, like the thorns in the story. Then the message about God cannot grow in them. Yet the good soil gives a splendid harvest, like people who are so glad about God they tell others too, and lead lives that please Him."

Another time, Jesus told this story.

Once there was a shepherd who had a hundred sheep. One day a sheep wandered off. When the shepherd counted his flock he found only ninety-nine sheep.

"One of my sheep is lost," he thought sadly. So he left the ninety-nine sheep and searched for the missing one until at last he found it. Filled with joy, he picked up the frightened animal, heaved in onto his strong shoulders, and carried it safely back to the flock. Then he led all his sheep to the fold. He called his friends, "Come on, everyone! Let's be happy together. My lost sheep is safely back in the fold."

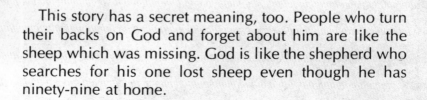

This story has a secret meaning, too. People who turn their backs on God and forget about him are like the sheep which was missing. God is like the shepherd who searches for his one lost sheep even though he has ninety-nine at home.

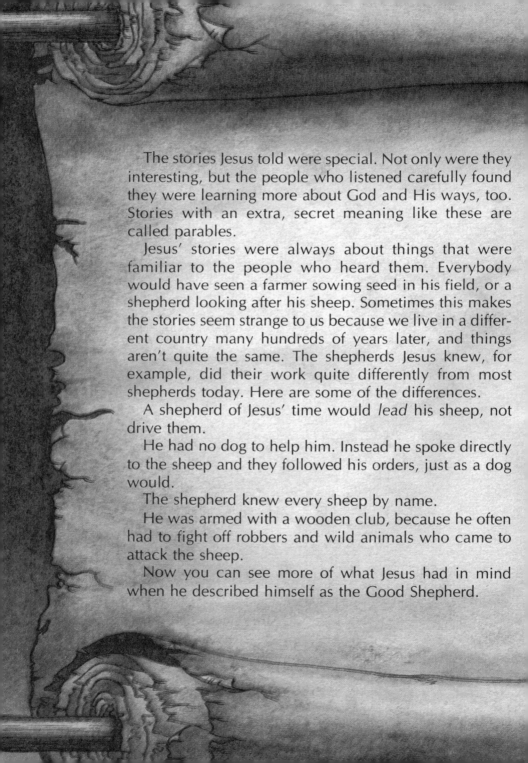

The stories Jesus told were special. Not only were they interesting, but the people who listened carefully found they were learning more about God and His ways, too. Stories with an extra, secret meaning like these are called parables.

Jesus' stories were always about things that were familiar to the people who heard them. Everybody would have seen a farmer sowing seed in his field, or a shepherd looking after his sheep. Sometimes this makes the stories seem strange to us because we live in a different country many hundreds of years later, and things aren't quite the same. The shepherds Jesus knew, for example, did their work quite differently from most shepherds today. Here are some of the differences.

A shepherd of Jesus' time would *lead* his sheep, not drive them.

He had no dog to help him. Instead he spoke directly to the sheep and they followed his orders, just as a dog would.

The shepherd knew every sheep by name.

He was armed with a wooden club, because he often had to fight off robbers and wild animals who came to attack the sheep.

Now you can see more of what Jesus had in mind when he described himself as the Good Shepherd.